Neurons Money

A practical method to live in prosperity

Ana Silvia Lara

BALBOA.PRESS
A DIVISION OF HAY HOUSE

Copyright © 2023 Ana Silvia Lara.

All rights reserved. No part of this book may be used or reproduced by any means, graphic, electronic, or mechanical, including photocopying, recording, taping or by any information storage retrieval system without the written permission of the author except in the case of brief quotations embodied in critical articles and reviews.

Balboa Press books may be ordered through booksellers or by contacting:

Balboa Press
A Division of Hay House
1663 Liberty Drive
Bloomington, IN 47403
www.balboapress.com
844-682-1282

Because of the dynamic nature of the Internet, any web addresses or links contained in this book may have changed since publication and may no longer be valid. The views expressed in this work are solely those of the author and do not necessarily reflect the views of the publisher, and the publisher hereby disclaims any responsibility for them.

The author of this book does not dispense medical advice or prescribe the use of any technique as a form of treatment for physical, emotional, or medical problems without the advice of a physician, either directly or indirectly. The intent of the author is only to offer information of a general nature to help you in your quest for emotional and spiritual well-being. In the event you use any of the information in this book for yourself, which is your constitutional right, the author and the publisher assume no responsibility for your actions.

Any people depicted in stock imagery provided by Getty Images are models, and such images are being used for illustrative purposes only. Certain stock imagery © Getty Images.

Interior Image Credit: CANVA

Print information available on the last page.

ISBN: 979-8-7652-4566-8 (sc)
ISBN: 979-8-7652-4565-1 (hc)
ISBN: 979-8-7652-4567-5 (e)

Library of Congress Control Number: 2023917980

Balboa Press rev. date: 09/22/2023

Dedicated to all who have been in search of answers, of something bigger...

CONTENTS

Acknowledgements ix
Prologue xi
Introduction xiii

Chapter 1   Money Cycle And Flow Formula 1
Chapter 2   Giving 23
Chapter 3   Neuronal Contraction 35
Chapter 4   Neuronal Expansion 43
Chapter 5   Time Cycles 53
Chapter 6   Formula Integration 59

Conclusion 77
Recommended Reading 81
Glossary 83
About The Author 85

ACKNOWLEDGEMENTS

Thank you all for being part of this book.

To everyone for the great contribution of which we are already part of the new Crystal Cities, the new humanity, the new consciousness expansion.

PROLOGUE

The six chapters that make up this book are assimilable for those people who have a broad vision towards the world and the energy it houses. An inexhaustible curiosity for knowledge and questions that need answering. This book proposes a new access to our interiority, a new perspective of the world and everything that surrounds it; as well as a different way to know more about oneself, starting with the soul.

Each of the chapters waits for its turn, with harmony and patience, to reveal valuable and light-filled information. The first chapter is an in-depth analysis of our beliefs, the way we routinely perceive life and the factors that make it up; It helps us to reflect on points that we simply do not question anymore because we decided to follow a path traced by all those who preceded us; leaving little room for a new view or meaning of things as it is, in this book, money.

The second chapter is an essential part, and can be interpreted as the heart, since it speaks of an essential theme that shapes the whole work. Giving is a concept that can change a person completely, its understanding can enlighten and guide the mind towards a new vision of reality.

The third chapter contributes even more, diving into neuronal contraction, described in detail to achieve a quick understanding.

The fourth chapter acts as a perfect complement, as it focuses on neuronal expansion, as well as one of the most intriguing topics that can be addressed: observer acts.

The fifth chapter, on the other hand, can be considered as the entrance to a new general perspective, since the time cycles expose, together with these realities, a path towards the awareness of what exists around us and how to manage it correctly.

Finally, in the sixth chapter an exhaustive inquiry is made about the formula and cycle of money and how it can be applied in different areas of life, especially in business, which is pleasantly useful for all who are willing to learn.

By Andrea Ramos

INTRODUCTION

You have ever wondered, how and where does the creation of money come from? Money is interrelated with another system, whether with health, partner, business, or work, everything. The disease is interrelated with the money part, since we have been taught that money is the circulating one, what we see as physical, as well as in material possessions. That is a form of representation of money.

Today we want to make money, we want to do well in prosperity, in finances, etc., but if we do not know what money is or how it works, which will make the network system begin to do a short-circuit caused by accumulation or what we believe as money.

Changing the chip about money has its degree of complexity. Let us understand how the money cycle works as neural fuel (energy source or gasoline) to make movements and adjustments, to integrate and understand the process of give-money-light. The view of money will be transformed to the great observer, which refers to money being a whole.

When talking about states and countries where there are billions of systems interrelated with money and in constant transformation, we will find an interrelation with health, well-being, illness, the relationship of couple, home, office, company, organizations, the environment, etc. On a global level everything is interrelated with the whole, until we understand this, we can say that we are understanding what money is.

An example would be being in a football or painting class, where money is interrelated to the family, in an event or circumstance. Did you find how many systems are interrelated in the field of money? What is the source from which these resources arrive?

What is your relationship to giving and receiving as the source of money? What means do you use to get the money in? The answer is the unlimited source of prosperity.

Money is light, but it is not light as we know it. It is about assembling the pieces from various angles, such as in the teaching of generating more income, where money is spoken of from accumulation or saving. If there is influence of the place where we are or live, there is an impact of up to 99.9% of the environment.

I started this book a few years ago when I moved to live in California. I mention this to emphasize that, for any event, movement, or adjustment there are three stages: before, during and after, as past, present, and future, in where the system prepares and accommodates this process of change, resulting in adjustments towards giving, which is network connection. This means that the system finds those high neural potentials or super brain capabilities and moves them to other places to reconnect the network. The result it has on the impact of the human being, both physical, mental, and emotional adjustments, as well as in all its manifestations.

Neuronal contraction is frequencies of fear, manipulation, trauma, judgment, expectations, among others. We can mention an example of a very abundant region where people react and live, that is, a percentage of the population that lives in some region X, connects with the energy or field of the place in where the network system is interfered by the vision of money and from the part of accumulation and material possession. In this system of networks, all the people who inhabit this region X, if they do not achieve their balance or stay in it, begin to connect with that neuronal contraction (state of judgment or expectations) and replicate everything that is in their container.

That is, people in that region begin to connect to that state of neuronal contraction, which is expectation and judgment. Then, they demand not being able to have a standard of living that occurs in this region X. Therefore, by not achieving and understanding of what money is or a full balance; they end up connecting with other network systems that are characterized by being in neuronal contraction, in which it is interfered by addictions, drugs, alcohol, among others.

Therefore, if there is a major influence of the environment towards you; In other words, where you are currently living influences your relationship with money. A person who is in country X is different from another person in country Y, the perspective of seeing money is vastly different. The systems are different, although we were all born in the same place or belong to the same family, we will be seeing that there is an impact of what the environment is towards us and influences directly.

Neuroscientists mention that 95% of what happens in the environment directly affects it, that is, what you feel has a relationship with the environment; It is very important to know that, if you cannot keep in balance, you will be connecting with other networks that are known as systems crossing (also called neural traffic), which are interrelated with other systems.

There are many indicators that help to find if there is a crossing system through symptomatology and pathology; Both help reveal this information. In addition, there is also an influence of the people who are around us or with whom we are connected, such as the partner, family, friends, or environment. Everything influences us, our home, neighborhood, city, state, country. That is, having a decrease in our network system corresponds directly to the study of crossing system.

There are several factors that today are interrelated, that decide or influence our daily life and show the relationship between the neuronal potential in equilibrium and the amount of money to create the circuit: give-money-light. This means that people who have that super-brain ability (superior ability), by not fueling up to repair their neurons and networked circuits; They may be experiencing neural resets or rewiring without any understanding. This can lead to the deterioration of physical, mental, emotional health, the relationship with the environment, the company, business and especially the relationship with money.

Even if you get to this region x from a process of imbalance, what happens is that they will connect with the crossings system, because all those systems are interfered with by others; They will connect or live their life experience from what those fields have. These same crossings are characterized by extreme doubt, confusion, expectation, judgment, betrayal, manipulation, deceit, fear, etc. If you are not aware of what is happening, it may be replicated repeatedly in various situations of life, giving way to a cycle. The only way to achieve your balance and support it is to keep a state of harmony and balance heart-brain-intestines-tailbone. The latter have a direct relationship with the amount of light - money.

Therefore, the key to living abundantly, in a place with an interfered system in the sense of accumulation and possession; It is to understand through knowledge, how the give-money-light cycle works. Since the latter, as a piece that assembles the puzzle, if it is not understood it can connect with neuronal contraction, where there is stress, pressure, anxiety, frustration, and confusion of what money is. All this leads to living in other situations, events, and increasingly stronger circumstances.

The interesting thing is to understand how to stay towards the great observer or state of harmony, regardless of where you live.

Since, by the theory of neural networks, the interrelation or crossing of systems will never cease to exist. The great challenge is to be happy and live in prosperity, regardless of the situation in the environment, family, work, or professional situation. We must see chaos as a possibility and transform it into a life full of fullness and harmony.

CHAPTER 1

MONEY CYCLE AND FLOW FORMULA

This book proposes the method to live in prosperity, in an interactive, practical, applicable, and demonstrable way, integrating the formula of the cycle and flow of money with the intention that it works as a neural fuel (source of energy or gasoline) and voltage adjusters to calibrate the connection points of network systems. Through this neural fuel, you create a new lifestyle, a new state of harmony, which allows you to live in prosperity.

Start integrating this method through the components of the money cycle and flow formula:

Method Integration

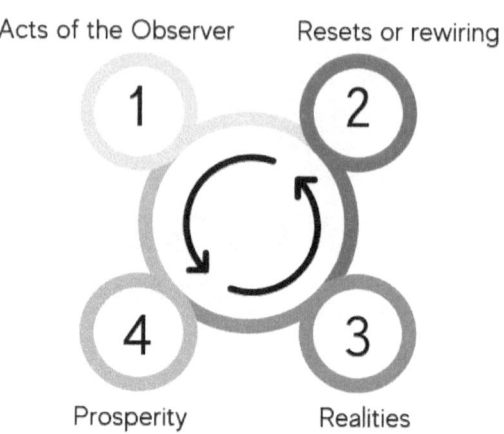

To do this, access this QR code that will take you to listen to the corresponding audios that are part of the formula and throughout the development of this book you will find each audio with the corresponding explanation:

- Observer acts
- Resetting & Rewiring
- Realities
- Prosperity

In method develops each part of the formula:

• **Money** = Giving (network connection) + neural expansion + time cycles

••• Giving: is the cycle and principle of giving, also called network connection

••• Neuronal expansion: creates the give-money-light circuit

••• Time cycles: integrates the 5 realities or 5 acts towards the great observer

For this, choose a nice space and answer for yourself these questions:

1	Do you know the definition of money in your life?
2	Does giving and sharing create a feeling, thought or emotion in you?
3	Do you know what the purpose of your giving is?
4	Do you connect with the give-money-light loop?
5	Is what you are currently doing aligned with giving and sharing?
6	Do you give and share in your daily life?

Upon completion of this exercise, the system makes the adjustments that each one needs to integrate the formula of the cycle and flow of money, which is understood as follows: money equals giving (network connection), plus expansion, plus the cycles of time. Understand giving, which is not as it is known, because giving is the network connection and this, in turn, has its degree or levels of complexity. Therefore, it is a constant and continuous process, in which it is integrated into this method...

Money is also called neurons from the perspective of the great observer, so you must understand that money is equal to the amount of light proportional to neuronal potential. It is not understood this way in daily life since money is simply seen as circulating and life revolves around it; by understanding it as something physical.

Therefore, ask yourself the following questions: Have you seen yourself and thought about what beliefs you have about money? When you give, whether it is some service or product,

What is your relationship to giving? From what emotion are you connecting with that process of giving? Have you ever wondered how much light or love a certain product/service cost?

The scope for this understanding is remarkably high when imagining how many neurons could be transformed by our thinking and integrating the definition of money. The language of words is light and neurons. The brain processes and integrates this new language that helps to assimilate what is lived, without striving to understand what is happening. Through this method, life experiences will be from the state of harmony, understanding and equanimity.

It is complex to talk about the possibility of changing the chip about the definition of accumulation and saving of money, this is something that has been seen throughout the history of humanity. It is difficult to open the understanding of something new, of a theory about money, because this theory comes to progressively transform and change that belief system. It is a process that is worked on the fly, without bringing attention to the results, but integrating this method day by day, the results will show up and take care of themselves without self-demand, judgments, and expectations.

If it is exemplified as a big cake; Sometimes we simply eat a small part when not everything has been tasted, or the understanding of theory and practice has not been unified. As neural potential evolves, new possibilities open, opportunities, roads, fields, systems. It is for this reason that the perspective and definition of money has evolved and each time we share it the understanding expands.

To know the secret to achieving fullness and prosperity is to know the full balance, it is possible to achieve the understanding of the triad: to give-money-light and to have a better quality of life in balance. Considering that this full process is interrelated with neural network systems, and these are supplied by neural fuels to create new circuits and achieve that balance in give-money-light.

The cycle and flow of money creates the circuit: give-money-light and is related to the neural network system; family or entrepreneurial and business roles can influence the flow of money, both defined and undefined or integrated roles.

NEURAL NETWORK SYSTEM

>Everything is a system of networks, everything is interrelated.

ANA LARA

The human being is more than a physical body, a set of micro and macro networks, all interrelated, that is, a set of systems interrelated with other systems, the great artistic and perfected machinery. Neural fuels create and generate brain biochemistry that repairs neural circuits.

The neural network system is composed of the set of cellular networks, neurons, neurotransmitters, and hormones up to the great universe; studies have revealed that neurons have been found in the heart and intestines. These network systems can yield information about the several types and movements of neural networks, effects, factors, components, and solutions to the corresponding system. Network systems include ancestral, cosmic, planetary, multiverse, universal, global, realities, lines, and times cycles.

The neuron is the vehicle and transmitter of light in the network system, achieving the interaction between neurons, brain and neural network systems, transmitter of information. There are billions of neurons in the human body, they function as detoxifiers, integrators, and adjusters of the network system environment, carrying information to the organs and systems of the body, forming, and creating new neurons that are connected and interconnected in the network systems.

The key is to keep the neurons alive, to keep the neuronal system moving, since the purpose is neurogenesis; the birth and restoration of new neurons, preventing neuronal death due to factors such as: oxidative stress, food, belief systems, addictions, drugs, among others

OBSERVER ACTS

We do not have to force these acts, simply let them be, even if some act is not verbally issued, we must be certain that it is happening. In the state of the great observer or 5th act, the same field shows and reveals how these acts act.

Acts change and transform, like the movement of a wave to be able to go towards the 5th act or 1st line of the flow and cycle of money. That is, there is a relationship between the acts of the observer and the lines of the flow and cycle of money. In this way, it evolves in a process that never ends, never culminates. These observer acts apply in your daily life; In any event, circumstance, situation, from the beginning and end of your day, in any area: personal, corporate, and business. Observer acts are:

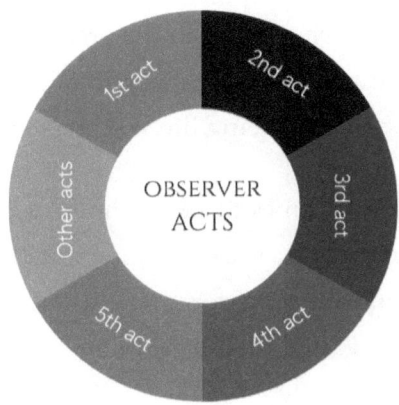

Act 1 integrates stress or physical body; This act is observing your breath; it is observing yourself from you.

Act 2 integrates stress or the emotional body, intestines; it is seeing yourself outside of yourself, as if you were outside yourself watching you.

Act 3 integrates stress or mental body (rational) and mind; it is watching you from a large mountain or waterfall.

Act 4 integrates the heart-brain-intestines, coccyx balance; It is to see yourself from the heart.

Act 5 integrates towards the heart-brain-intestines-coccyx balance; it is to see yourself in both directions, from the heart to the environment (outside) and from the environment to the heart, forming a large vortex from the heart.

The 4th and 5th act, allows receptive rewiring and integrated life experiences, this is anchoring from the great heart, which allows us to see the adjustments that are made in heart-brain-intestines, integrating a new way of seeing life with respect to money.

Observer acts work 3 times to reach the 5th act: before, during and after; In other words, it can be interpreted as past, present, and future, this means that, for every event, circumstance or situation, there is an "before, during or after". The purpose is to understand and integrate observer acts as a new consciousness in your daily life.

The formation of these pillars creates network connection, that is, light in neural network systems; fuel, which is essential for the generation and creation of circuits. Observer acts are related to the events you have lived, with the amount of light-money and with some characteristics of the formula such as: durability and long life in the time cycles; In addition, these life experiences could be considered as rewired.

Listen to the audio of the group session, *observer acts*, accessing the QR:

NEURAL RESETS OR REWIRING

A reset, rewiring, trauma, bioshock or short circuit can manifest itself in a death, illness, addictions, change of house, change of job, separation, divorce, etc., all those strong life experiences have a great impact on the balance with the heart-brain-intestines; to be able to integrate them is of great complexity if a repair or a restoration of the deterioration caused by the alterations of the neural network systems is not carried out.

If there is no supply of neural fuel to make the repairs or adjustments corresponding to these systems in deterioration or dysfunction can manifest itself in the physical, mental, emotional, energetic health, in relation to the couple, family, business, work and with the relationships of the environment in general. The great puzzle is to have a rewiring with the knowledge and access to neural fuels, this is the reason for the existence of this method that integrates the theory and practice of the flow and cycle of money, cycle of giving and sharing.

The resets, or rewiring, will continue as you move toward neuronal evolution, so you continue to have life experiences. However, this time from a full understanding, from the state of harmony; the recovery process will be more fluid towards full balance, in a different way to a person who does not receive fuel, who will show losses or deterioration in different areas of their life.

To the lack of corresponding neuronal fuel required by the brain, it presents some symptoms and corresponding pathology. Today, there are some fuels, but they are not enough given the evolution towards the super brain or 5th act require other types of fuels that are already accessible as this method allows you to stock up. Therefore, when the brain does not have the corresponding fuel, it presents short circuits, as if it were a Christmas tree where the lights stop being on and begin to turn off.

To keep the lights or connection points in the neural circuit on, in this book we propose the application of this method through the application of the formula to create the circle: give-money-light; it requires that the person is well supplied with neural fuel, because if it is not available, the network system itself will start to supply in order to achieve this balance. Its process is based on rewiring the neural network system and repairing distorted or deteriorated circuits to keep those bulbs on.

Some symptoms of being in neuronal contraction are feeling fed up, fear of not knowing where to go or feel doubt or extreme confusion, feeling that what we have done has not been worth it. An example to understand this is a car; If it does not have gasoline, it will not be able to work, so you have to find a way to stock up so that it works correctly, durably and lasts over time. That is why neural rewiring comes, which is based on strong life experiences, such as grief, illness, loss or death, experiences close to death, etc.

Make a list of the life experiences you have had in the last 3, 6 or 9 years, and how there is a relationship between each experience or event and the amount of money.

Life experiences occur for a greater purpose, and this is the way that the great system or great observer, state of harmony, balance, or coherence, performs to repair the circuits and can function. Adjustments and movements are made gradually, steadily, and continuously.

The purpose of supplying fuel is to set in motion or the correct functioning of the neural network system, that is, to the lack of fuel, the great machinery of networks has a slow fluid, to unlike if constantly and continuously every day it receives, integrates, or refuels (this method), the neural network system takes its own fluidity, rhythm, and movement.

There is a certain complexity in integrating information; in other words, it opens up the possibility of giving, receiving and sharing; Complete the cycle of giving in all directions to execute giving as a component of the formula; if you open your heart to give, receive and share, the result will be a total transformation from the sense of not accumulating money and starting to generate new neural connections. This is accessing the inexhaustible source of money. When the true concept of giving is integrated as a network, the flow of money will manifest itself in proportion to the amount of light emitted from the brain, in the network connection with the environment.

Reset or rewiring are the experiences, events, life circumstances that happen to the human being, these life teachings serve to adapt learning in today's life. As we have seen, understanding has its degree of complexity and is not easily achieved. The great system or great observer, as a state of consciousness, tests people to live and experience such rewiring. There are children, young people and adults with remarkably high neuron potential that require fuel and, when they are not receiving it, somehow, they must be done. This is where life experiences such as rewiring, resets, bioshock or short circuits arise.

Our education about money has been from accumulation or possession, but today everything has been transformed, the way, form, vision of understanding, applying, and living what money is. Let's understand the flow, creation, and generation of money from the perspective of the great observer or the state of coherence or harmony. What results, in understanding what money is without self-demand and expectation, since its true purpose is to generate light in a multiplied and expanded way, from the state of the great observer or state of harmony, understanding the money formula and cycle, because giving is the network connection and balancing of neural potential.

When think of money, think of the goal of well-being, security and as an accumulation or possession. In fact, the way that have experienced or lived money is from the sense of selfishness or separation. This information is in the systems and when they are interrelated with other systems, like systems crossings (neuronal traffic) are created.

The resetting or rewiring have a lot to do with and influence the system of neural networks, the latter looks how to supply itself before the replicity or continuity that is presented. The neuronal reset is related to the amount of money and light, to achieve this it is necessary to support balance and stop feeling that you have little or much, that you lack or spare; because it has to do with brain performance, harmonious and equanimous state.

Also, non-integrated rewiring can worsen insomnia, lack of balance and neurotransmitters, lack of oxygen in the blood, which has to do with neural resets. While the oxygenation of the blood is equal to neuronal resets:

OS = RN

Greater oxygenation – greater neuronal rewiring balance

Less oxygenation – lack of balance in neuronal rewiring

It is related to the number of connection points or bulbs on or off in the neural network system, in addition to having a relationship with the cycles of time. In the face of chaos, we must stop being so reactive and manage to go towards the state of harmony, the state of the great observer in the face of unexpected circumstances or events, chaos, conflict, trauma, among others. It is possible to achieve this, because when you find yourself in some situation of chaos, there is a lot of clarity in turn; it is a moment of transition that takes a few seconds to direct or swing towards observer acts, this is also the connection: brain-heart-intestines.

Rewiring allows *you to "see the moment clearly, without judgment or expectation."* Perfection in clarity is the great observer, acting in the moment that is, because when the observer investigates chaos, he cannot intervene, as if he had to stay to take the next step and, in that way, enter the field. The observer contemplates those seconds of chaos as if time stopped, and he does so to see the equanimity and impeccability of the act. Without judgment and expectation, they show the entrance to the field in tranquility and serenity.

It is there that the great observer acts to culminate the act.

The neural network system works through neural fuels so that your corresponding system balances and stops replicating. In addition, it works at the level of the nervous system, balancing the altered states of sleep, stress, anxiety, and neurotransmitters, achieving physical, mental, and emotional balance.

Through the following diagram the rewiring or neural resets are represented. These rewired are life experiences such as **NDE** (near-death experiences), trauma, deaths, separation, divorce, illness, job loss, change of home or job, drugs, addictions, among others.

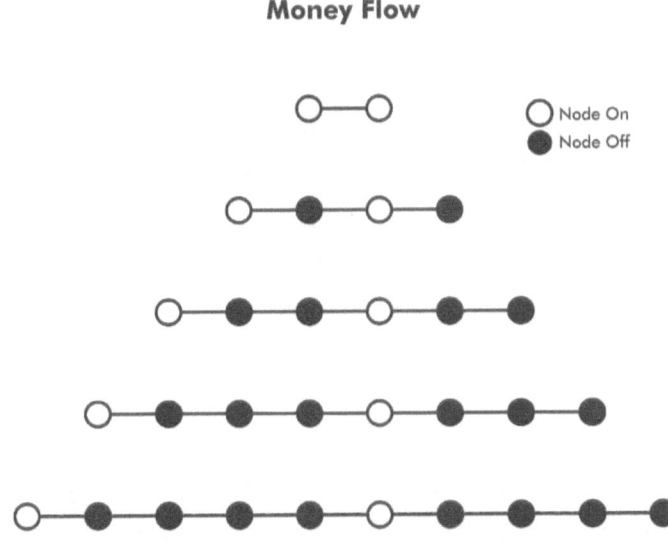

Money flow

Notice in the previous image, there are five lines that form a system of neural networks where there are circles that represent the connection points or lights. The blank circles are the lights on, and the black circles are the dull spotlights. These five lines relate to the five observer acts. There is a synchronicity with neural flow and money flow.

Today the vision of money for the network system has been transformed and leads us to integrate the new definition and perspective of money based on the flow, cycle, creation, and origin of money that is created from the great network system and not from accumulation or savings.

Therefore, a person who remains with a balanced circuit and supplying neural fuel constantly will result in the amount of light and the amount of money that is manifesting. The 5th act also called the state of harmony, state of the great observer, equanimity, super brain, great network system, among others. Case studies show different neural circuits of a group of people and these reveal that there is a relationship with the cycles of time, where 1, 2 or 3 resets are found at the same time. Network connection is decisive, since it can vary for each neural potential of people since it depends on the level of balance that you can support in your daily life.

From the previous image we can see that it represents the circuits and circles as a connection point or lights as follows:

- 1st line: on, on, corresponds to the 5th act.
- 2nd line: on, off, on, off, corresponds to the 4th act; people present manifestations, symptoms, or pathologies to a low level, which begins to diminish physically, mentally, emotionally.

- 3rd line: on, off, off, on, off, off, on, corresponds to a 3rd act, present symptoms, and pathologies at a moderately important level and in different situations or circumstances.
- 4th line: on, off, off, off, on, off, off, off, on, corresponds to a 2nd act; They present symptoms at an advanced level, such as sleep disturbance, diseases, imbalance in heart-brain-intestines-coccyx and begin to manifest the lack of neuronal fuel by all the foci turned off.
- 5th line: on, off, off, off, off, on, off, off, off, off, on, this corresponds to a 1st act; People have super advanced symptoms or diseases.

There is a relationship between observer acts and the lines of the flow and cycle of money, as seen in the following image:

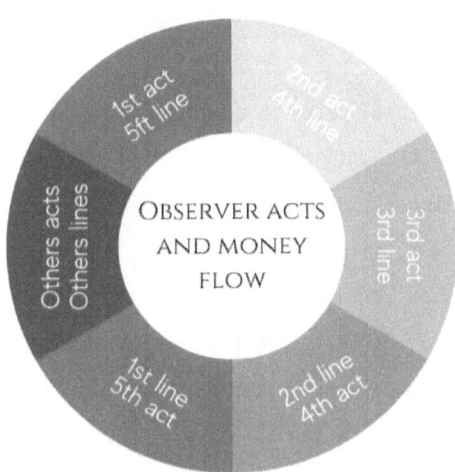

Between the 3rd and 4th line the mental gaps begin. People who feel they lose things, unfocused, feel stuck, disabled, not knowing where to go; It is where they begin to diminish on a physical, mental, or emotional level. There are people who suffer from more advanced diseases and are in the 4th and 5th line, remembering that this last line is, practically, the appearance of various neurological, psychiatric, and psychological diseases, among others. We usually see people very normally, but they are between the 4th and 5th line. This shows that there is a relationship between these lines, the amount of light and money.

Network connection or giving cycle with brain-heart-intestines that can maintain a person with superior abilities even when not supplied with fuel required to Repairing these neural circuits, can fall to a 3rd or 4th line, which will cause a deterioration of your health at several levels such as: physical, mental, emotional, energetic, until you reach the deepest levels of neuronal contraction, and this is also the 5th line.

There are signs that more advanced fueling is needed to repair connection points or bulbs in neural network systems, this can be revealed by integration of the acts of the observer. That is, the fuel required for each person or the voltage levels of light that functions as fuel to be measured and will be reflected by the integration of the observer acts towards the great observer and the realities. Therefore, this method integrates this into its components. Keeping those spotlights on in the neural network system translates into balance.

When the field detects that there is no fuel supply and that it is not in balance give-money-light, that fuel is injected through life experiences, (of those neural rewiring to create the circuit: give-light-money), circuits or bridges of connection in equilibrium of the neural network system, depending on the supply of neural fuel.

A rewiring can be exemplified as when you open a water hose, it comes out with all the force that carries the electric current of the water and that is transmitted to your brain, specifically to your neural network, this can cause imbalance because there is no control in the amount of light or electrical current that is reaching the brain so it can cause deterioration or distortions in neural circuits.

This occurs for resets or rewiring in imbalance of neuronal potential and presents as strong life experiences, and this has a replication with the connection with other people, places, and animals.

Light or electrical current that is reaching the brain so it can cause deterioration or distortions in neural circuits. This occurs for resets or rewiring in imbalance of neuronal potential and presents as strong life experiences, and this has a replication with the connection with other people, places, and animals.

This can happen to children, young people and adults with extraordinary talents and abilities when they cannot supply themselves and support their neuronal potential in balance, begins to decrease in them and present symptoms in physical, mental, emotional and over everything in the environment. Since there is no fuel, it will have to stop there; Because adjustments have to be made in your system, family nucleus or the systems in which you are interrelated such as central nervous system, immune system, circulatory system, among others. Depending on what life experiences you have had, there will be events that supply the signs that characterize these memories.

Here are some symptoms of neural rewiring:

- Choking or lack of oxygen
- Extreme tiredness
- Feeling lost or with no way out
- Lack of memory and concentration sleep disturbance
- Imbalance in the following indicators: blood pressure, heart rate or rhythm, blood oxygenation, etc.
- Various symptoms and pathology depend on neuronal potential.

You must understand the process that is being integrated and the rest we leave to the great observer who is part of the rewiring as a function of time.

Some benefits of having a rewiring in balance and sustained by neural fuel are:

- Improves active sex life.
- Wakefulness is balanced improved sleep status and quality.
- Increase in memory.
- Greater creativity
- Sensitivity is balanced, acting as a ray of light in the heart. It can last from 1 to 3 days.

INTEGRATING REWIRING

Make 2 personal and family timelines, you can take the last 3, 6, 9 or 12 years.

FAMILY OR PERSONAL TIMELINE

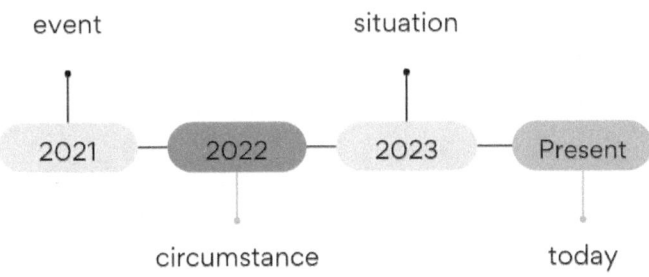

Neural resets and rewiring

Neural resets and rewiring

- A personal line to work on life experiences such as deaths, illnesses, change of house, work, partner, divorce.
- The other timeline is familiar in relation to the father and mother.

That is, while these events, circumstances and situations happened, there could be a decrease for money and light because the network system tried to supply through that event, circumstance, or situation, that's why it created that bioshock, short circuit, rewiring, resetting, etc. Write the teaching of each event, circumstance, or situation you have experienced, and make the personal or family timeline that will be integrated, being an observer of your own timeline.

Money has a relationship with the balance connection with brain-heart-intestines-coccyx and heart with central crystal of mother earth.

Achieve the balance or state or harmony or great observer, it is necessary to integrate the mother and the father, feminine and masculine principle. This is the reason the line of the family system is worked in relation to the father and the mother.

Listen to the following audio of the group session: rewiring or resets; accessing the QR:

CHAPTER 2

GIVING

Giving is the vehicle, engine, motive, foundation, mechanism, or natural fuel to repair deterioration in the neural network system. The vehicle of giving, detached from judgments, expectations, structures, beliefs, etc. The capacity of giving is in the brain, that is, the process of giving is like an energy circuit that is connected from the heart to the cerebral hemispheres and this cycle of giving can be affected by the n+1 field (this is the way to call the sum of all fields). The cycle of giving can affect or impair the behavior of cells and neurons, added to oxidative stress and others that can cause neuronal death, this if it is conducted from conditioning or expectations. For what it now gives, without generating expectation of its return, since it will arrive in many ways, forms, and people. What you stop receiving on the one hand comes to you on the other hand, the field or system handles compensating the process of giving.

The neural network system and the super brain are networked. That is, giving is equal to brain ability, neuronal potential, and the connection between heart-brain-intestines-coccyx. The cycle of giving is also related to the cerebral hemispheres and neural network systems, as well as to the feminine principle, mother earth Gaia. Giving is an engine to create fuel and to give continuity to the repair of circuits in neural network systems.

Human giving can be described as pieces that put together the big puzzle, it seems very simple, but when it is really coming together, we will be able to see giving in its different perspectives and really understand the concept of what network connection is, but to get to that point, we first have to lay the foundations. Integrate the construction of the cycle of giving and sharing in your day to day, even when we do not understand what network connection is, which is to be connected all in a system and how situations, events and circumstances are replicated. The method requires the cycle of giving because without it cannot work; therefore, rewiring and resets are originated to repair the neural circuit.

It is sometimes thought that natural fuel is giving out, but that can cause a serious imbalance. Therefore, it is important to understand how this process works.

For example, when you go to the cinema, the first thing you give is the ticket to go into see the movie. This would work in real life, giving before receiving, regardless of whether you liked it or not at the end of watching it, you have already given, and this fulfills the cycle of giving. It happens that sometimes in daily life it works differently because you connect with *"if I like the movie I'm living, I'm going to give, and if I don't like it, I'm not going to give."* It gives like going to the movies, that is, it gives like the entrance to the cinema. Giving light before receiving is light itself, as in the cinema you give before seeing the film, usually the human being gives after seeing the film, this leads to judgment, expectation, criticism, justification for not giving, etc. This is where a burden is generated by giving, the counterpart of the process of giving.

It is like the entrance to the cinema, in every step of your life and what you will find will be something extraordinary. The joy of giving is light, and giving is the joy of receiving without judgment or expectation. Take the photo before entering the cinema and that image is joy and gladness, which is light, apply it to everything. Give the entrance to the cinema and in each stage or area of your life, give the entrance to the cinema and enjoy the function. Giving before watching the movie generates oxytocin in the brain, which is the love hormone, as well as generates serotonin, etc. Giving balances and releases your neurotransmitters.

The feeling of joy before receiving is the greatest act you have to give, maintain and balance towards the great observer, given the intention or mechanism and cycle of giving, and what you do. It generates a harmonious equanimous state.

Remember that human giving is when we begin to map and cycle giving. What this method suggests when integrating giving, is to connect every day, with that space of joy that created you to go to the movies and that satisfaction to share it with the environment, because of the process of giving; When you understand it, you begin to build the basis of the cycle of giving, which is properly to work this method to integrate the formula and create the circuit: give-money-light.

It is possible to transform and renew your life, achieving that balance in neuronal potential and if the theory is fulfilled, it is possible that what is given without judgment and expectation will return multiplied. However, the essential thing is to follow what the field requires, to understand that this is also how life and cycles work.

Talking about the cycle of giving as natural fuel for our brain, is also to achieve the balance of heart-brain-intestines-coccyx; It is to set in motion the natural fuel of giving in all the acts of our life. Sometimes, the brain does not understand how the process of giving works and the benefits it obtains by supplying itself with this natural fuel that will generate the balance of neurotransmitters such as oxytocin (which is the hormone of love), serotonin, etc. This fuel helps balance neurotransmitters by making neural network adjustments. On the other hand, there is the counterpart; where people, when they do not have this natural fuel of giving, it is difficult or complex to understand this process to achieve balance.

As mentioned before, to integrate this method into the day to day has its degrees of complexity but there is continuity to achieve full balance. In other words, giving is the joy of receiving, giving gives you joy to receive without judgment or expectation. Today, there are people who have many expectations and judgments. Brain evolution is advancing rapidly, and the presence of environmental factors shows that it requires new fuels such as the cycle of giving because in the absence of these, it can begin to short-circuit.

There are some natural fuels such as connection with the forest, contact with nature, connection with the water of the oceans, the five elements, the sun, the moon, etc. These fuels also help our cerebral hemispheres and the cycle of giving. Today we have this method that works the formula of the cycle and flow of money, which supplies the neural fuel to repair our neural network system and keep us in balance. If we work this method in a constant, continuous, and progressive way we can have a better quality of life, integrating judgments and expectations, generating a multiplier effect of the cycle of giving.

All this is related to money, and it is not easy to change our chip; either by the whole belief system inserted into our genetic code, we take the amount of money as the circulating and for this method money is a state of harmony, of full balance. So, it is not properly the amount of light that will define that you are in abundance or that things are fine, but the amount of light.

The important thing is to know that, when projects do not occur, it is because they are not aligned in the intentions of the cycle of giving and network connection. The cycle of giving is an energy or sensation that we are experiencing in the form of happiness, harmony, and fulfillment in brain-heart connection. Although, it must be mentioned that the cycle of giving in this way is complex, because there are many judgments, expectations and that is what breaks the cycle.

It is necessary to unite all those pieces that form the giving and, only in this way, this cycle can be fulfilled. It is a human condition to be selfish, to have judgments and expectations. We have seen that only 3% of the population can generate this fuel naturally, so it is difficult to keep neuronal power in balance.

This method refers to the fact that the cycle of giving is network connection. We have a concept about giving, which is programmed primarily by expectations and judgments about giving expecting something in return. That is, giving is related to conditioning, so it does not occur in a natural way, because such a condition is so anchored in our programming that we need to leave that network and connect to the cycle of giving and sharing from the state of harmony. It requires connecting with giving from a generous and kind heart. Although it is complex to work with this natural fuel, it is essential to start building it from the base of giving to what is the network connection.

Today they talk about earning enormous amounts of money or refer to money based on quantity and accumulation; what is questioned is how money (light) is created if the flow and cycle of it is not known. Although money is arriving as circulating, it can leak and cease to be durable and lasting over time, since there will be situations in which the process of giving is not fully sustained, aligned, and anchored with the flow and cycle of money to create the circuit: give-money-light.

It is important to understand it, because the money that is the given known network connection in the formula, has more than a representation in the form of physical circulation. Therefore, we must understand how this formula works and integrate the method into our daily lives, as a generator and creator of the give-money-light circuit in a fluid way.

Sometimes it is believed that you save, when what happens is that you stop giving, therefore, the part of the savings does not apply under this formula. The perspective of giving is adjusting and will see how to compensate for all these processes in a balanced way. Neural rewiring also occurs when there is loss of money, that is, there is a relationship between money and events, or strong life circumstances called rewiring or neural resets.

Talking about saving, it is time to give, both money and light will never be lacking. That is, there will always be a supply of light and money, resources, provisions, and it will be in such an extraordinary way that you will enjoy it.

Of course, considering the characteristics of this formula such as durability, durability, ease, neutrality, happiness, prosperity, health, among others. Achieving maintenance and going towards a 5th act or state of harmony, allows the corresponding adjustments to be made, since the person does not interfere and intervenes in anything of what happens if you remain in this state of coherence, harmony, equanimity, is more let the corresponding thing happen. Likewise, the definitions and concepts of business, couple, friendship, in relation to the process of giving have been transformed.

However, it has been revealed in the cycle of giving the inheritances of the father or mother. This is related as adjustments are made in their family and business systems, adjustments also come of concepts, people, events, and circumstances.

The way in which love, the couple, friendship is perceived is very different as observed from the state of the great observer or 5th act, so a transformation of the system and the entire environment comes.

There are many events or circumstances that are happening and that you are currently living since the human being requires other types of fuels to be able to sustain and support the neuronal potential so high, so this method is revealed to achieve living in prosperity. The human being is like a supercomputer, has an extraordinary ability to live in happiness and lasting and enduring prosperity through all time.

There is a prelude to working this method, where through the signs that are presented, you can perceive and understand what has been required to move to the next step or new level of consciousness and go to the 5th act, the new state of balance, the great observer, the state of harmony.

It has been seen that natural fuel only manages to integrate 3 to 7% of the population due to the super high neuronal potential or super brain capabilities.

The fuel itself requires the use of other technologies that perform the integration of rewiring at the level of neural networks, so that it is possible to make way for balanced network connection;

For this reason, this method was born to reach beyond 7% of the population and cover 93% of the world's population.

People usually want and crave to see results. Therefore, giving is like the pearl of the great price, which may be impossible to achieve, but today with knowledge it is possible to achieve the giving known as network connection. Understanding is achieved when theory is applied in daily practice.

NETWORK CONNECTION

You are the great vortex heart that creates the network connection; what is needed to achieve it is to supply the neural circuits, that all lights are turned on, since they may have several circuits turned off. To support balance is to keep the continuous flow of the circuit: give-money-light.

That is, to stay on the diagram of the flow and cycle of money, in the 2nd line, which is circuit on and off, within normal levels towards full equilibrium.

The neural network system will require amount and balance of light, since it is not possible to generate it naturally, so the amount of fuel is insufficient for the brain and the consequence is that rewiring and resets. Given this, it can deteriorate in physical, mental, emotional, energetic health and go to a 3rd line of the flow diagram and cycle of money, where it begins to deteriorate.

The 5th line already exists, they are difficult and complex processes, in which you have to be supplying the fuel every day, currently you can do it through this method working constantly. When certain pathologies or diseases appear, the degree of complexity increases, and this is due to an endless number of factors. The intention is to support balance in the 1st line that integrates the 5th act to create the circuit: give-money-light and connect in network, to achieve heart-brain-intestines coherence, this is the full balance, the state of harmony, great observer.

TRANSFORMATIVE LANGUAGE

This language rewires the brain and anchors it in the field, materializing in your daily life. In addition, you can integrate daily the characteristics or principles of this method of the flow and cycle of money, which are all the words that end in "ity", which is synonymous with Light. Here are some examples of words that end in "ity":

- Durability
- Neutrality
- Prosperity
- Neuroplasticity
- Serenity
- Security
- Tranquility
- Fertility
- Fidelity

Use language presently, feeling and seeing, with all certainty that it already is, example:

Prosperity is already.
Prosperity is already in me.
Prosperity is already in me, it is already.
Prosperity is already in me, so it is.
Thank you, thank you, thank you.

Close the sentence with gratitude, example:

Thank you, thank you, thank you.

Make a list every day at the beginning and end of your day, words that end in "ity" that resonate in you, in your heart, and in this way, you will be integrating the transformative language in an ongoing way.

Also, there is a transformation in our language, this also influences to integrate the flow of money, so it transforms from this moment:

      Save, Cut ------------ Give

      Decrease ------------- Share and expand

      Healing -------------- Integration

      Observer ------------- Healer

      Therapy---------------Session

CHAPTER 3

NEURONAL CONTRACTION

The degree of distortion of reality has to do with addictions. The post-traumatic effect of various events and circumstances, caused by the crossings of systems characterized by fear, panic, uncertainty and distortion of reality; has done great neuronal damage resulting in people with high levels of depression, anxiety, stress post-traumatic, sleep disturbance due to the central nervous system, increased body temperature, blood pressure and heart rhythm irregularity.

The impact translates into physical, mental, emotional, economic, financial, work, professional and business stress; These people are characterized by not giving continuity and culmination to their projects in their relationships with the environment; whether family, company, or business. They do not make their life plan in a coherent, constant, continuous, and progressive way.

This manifest low productivity and other diseases due to lack of neural fuel.

Today, people with neural super potential or super brain, possess great talents, gifts, and abilities, whether artistic, culinary, sports, scientific or genius capabilities that, to the lack of neural fuel required to supply their neural network system and achieving balance, cerebral coherence, cardiac or state of harmony, can present various neural rewiring. Known as bioshock or short circuits in your network system. That is, neuronal transmission or signaling ceases to be continuous, so it is also interfered with due to numerous factors that caused these resets, such as the presence of addictions, drugs, near-death experiences, belief systems, stress, among others.

Therefore, the person may stop staying in balance and present alteration of the central nervous system and low frequency towards neuronal contraction, resulting in the great neuronal rewiring. That is, a greater number of neuronal short circuits, more relationship with addictions, diseases, and neuronal contraction. This is disease, creating separation or distortion of reality.

The absence of neural fuel creates neuronal contraction and, in turn, generates an addiction because people look to counteract anxiety, leading them to relapse into alcohol, drugs and other addictions.

Therefore, to stop repeating things is to continuously supply neural fuel, it is to integrate and work continuously with this method to achieve balance and network connection. This is the cycle of giving and, in turn, the flow and cycle of money.

Usually, people without neural fuel supply connect with neural contraction networks, which are divided into several degrees. People who have this contraction are characterized by being intolerant, they manage to get confused, they reject, they feel attacked when you speak to them with the truth, they feel criticized, judged, crowded, stressed, they do not accept what other people tell them.

From the following list of symptoms, look at which ones you have perceived or felt in the last 3, 6, 9 or 12 months and make a list and find some of the following symptoms of neuronal contraction:

- Economic stress
- Work and professional stress
- Low productivity
- Suicides
- Diseases, anxiety, depression
- Sleep disturbance fatigue
- Excessive tiredness
- Doubt
- Confusion
- Uncertainty
- Manipulation
- Fear
- Passive
- Distortion
- Increased body temperature
- Increased blood pressure
- Heart rhythm irregularity
- Muscle spasms

- Insomnia
- Lack of balance of neurotransmitters
- Lack of oxygen in the blood
- Power struggles to "cede power"
- Undeclared wars.
- Manipulation game imposition
- Obligation
- Selfishness
- Drugs and addictions

Systems crossing (neuronal traffic) can present as a disease. Neuronal contraction, which is the counterpart of neuronal expansion, will manifest itself in symptoms and pathology, such as alteration of the central nervous system. The brain will be on alert all the time, which leads to sleep disturbance. Today, there are many indicators that reveal this neuronal contraction such as: oxygenation in the blood, heart rate or rhythm, blood pressure, among others.

Examples of neural contraction are the creation of judgments and expectations about money, comparing oneself with other people, among others. If it is not possible to stay in balance, the brain will always relate to systems crossing, which will be depleting the neural network system, and this translates into the deterioration of physical, mental, emotional, and energetic health. Money can also cause imbalance by being connected to judgments and expectations, although the vision of money is progressively transforming today.

It has been seen that, in some relationships where both have extraordinary genius capacities; one person is in expansion and the other in neuronal contraction, which is described as processes difficult. The contraction comes from the 3rd line to the 5th line of the money cycle and flow diagram.

This means that, when in contact with the partner, environment, children, family, friends, company, or business, it can present systems crossing or neuronal contraction, having a very high degree of complexity because there will be a decrease, this is manifested in the appearance of symptoms and pathologies because of the neuronal contraction that these people are living. People who are in this contraction, even if they have all the neural potential, genius, and superior abilities, will not be able to sustain themselves if there is no fuel supply towards equilibrium and they will be moving towards neuronal contraction.

The theory says that, to support and create the circuit give-money-light, the person must remain in that balance based on theoretical, practical knowledge and fuel supply, the balance of the give cycle and networking. It is possible that people who are in neuronal contraction transform towards expansion, and this is to enjoy a state of full balance.

SYSTEMS CROSSING

Also called neuronal traffic, it refers to connecting to a network x, y or z; starting from there the point of intersection originates to connect with other alternate networks, such as neural contraction networks such as: co-vid, addictions, drugs, among others.

When you work with this method, you gain the understanding that there is always light, just like the currents of electric light that are in motion all the time. That means that there are amounts of light and money all the time being built under this theory. If we want to have enormous amounts of money and be abundant, natural fuel is not enough, neural fuels are needed to disengage us from those networks that are crossroads of systems.

To exemplify, systems crossing is the crossing of several threads of different colors, which are entangled or tied to form a network of several threads; this is a system crossing, which can also be altered due to other fields or interrelated systems. The interrelation with other systems means that we cannot stay in automatic balance, our brain will be hooked with what it finds, networks in neuronal contraction, as mentioned above.

The neural fuel that is applied when integrating this method into your daily life leads the brain to gamma waves, where the processes of adjustments are made, as well as repairing neural networks or circuits, to achieve go towards the 5th act or state of harmony, state of the great observer or great network system. So, by working continuously this method, it means fueling and this, in turn, can disconnect from those networks that form a crossroads of systems and reconnect to their original state, the state of harmony, equanimity, without chaos, in a subtle and harmonious way. It is possible that people perceive the symptoms and various pathologies at the physical, mental, and emotional level because of connecting with neuronal contraction, that is, when they connect to another networks like systems crossing.

The important thing is to work this method, so that this movement and fluidity can be generated; the flow of money, open the field and begin to create the circuit give-money-light.

To reach that we need to achieve understanding and that adjustments are made at the neural level and integrate the concept of accumulation, because accumulating money does not apply to the accumulation of light; it is not possible to accumulate light.

The light is to get rid of those concepts in which we have lived, that whole system of beliefs about money and understand more about a process that is in motion and that will never lack money, because it is like saying that there is a lack of light, and this is not possible since we are in constant flow and movement of light all the time, that is, continuously, constantly, progressively, forming the pieces of the formula that make up this method.

CHAPTER 4

NEURONAL EXPANSION

It means when the brain is in balance with the ability of super brain or neural super potential, in connection and coherence with the heart-brain-intestines. In addition, variables such as the systems crossing (neuronal traffic) and the neural networks system, also called expansion, are integrated.

The brain can encompass all network systems, even the point of origin of the great system itself, but everything depends on the balance with the neuronal potential. The great observer is a state of consciousness, it is seen through the eyes of the heart, it is also called a great networks system, that connects with the multiple realities. Therefore, coexisting in other realities is also neuronal expansion.

DNA

The brain creates new connections, generating new neural circuits. Network systems connected to the various fields strengthen DNA patterns to achieve a new consciousness. That is, DNA is the watershed for neuronal expansion, the spearhead, the catalyst, controller, generator of neural network systems, the great designer of neural network systems, creator of new systems called great networks system or great observer.

The expansion goes from macro level to micro, multiverses, macro networks, in similarity to the functioning of the brain, neural networks, connection with neurotransmitters, levels of oxygenation in the blood and hemoglobin; until reaching protons, neutrons, electrons, the nucleus of the cell and from there to mitochondrial DNA. The neuronal expansion is explained through mitochondrial DNA, the great connection, the return to the origin, the Fibonacci; it shows that the brain can achieve the network connection and acquire the super brain capacity, this is the 5th act, it is the totality of all realities happening at the same time.

The great machinery of DNA and its relationship with the central nervous system is that of replicator and transformer of neural network systems. It can create new nerve connections and neuroplasticity, through which new neural circuits are created.

To increase neuroplasticity, neuronal fuels are needed, which handle repairing the circuits to achieve proper functioning and maintain neuronal connection and communication; it also balances the oxidative stress, promoting the regeneration and birth of new neurons (neurogenesis). Its impact comes from the genome to repair chromosomes; It can also correct the strands of mitochondrial DNA and its metabolism.

The interesting thing is to see that belief systems are lodged even from DNA.

Look at your family tree and answer these questions for you:

- How many generations are there in your family system?
- How many beliefs do you have about money?
- What beliefs do your parents, families, and environment have about money that influences you?

COMMUNICATION AND NEURAL CONNECTION

It is related to the connection of the brain and the neural networks system in the time cycles; It is the communication between neurons and brains, as well as the interaction of the great field or towards the 5th act. The latter is also called, the great observer is the giving in network, the neural potentials in balance, there occurs the healing or integration. People who manage to go towards neuronal expansion or great observer and stay in balance, they create the circuit: give-money-light; that is, to live in prosperity.

If the flow of money has to do with our neural networks system, it means that, at the time of being fueled, these are destined for the creation of those neurons or for the creation of light. If it is kept in balance, in constant movement and structural adjustment of the body, it will allow neuronal expansion to be achieved throughout the environment.

The lack of neural fuel tends to become a problem, as the natural creation of fuel is not enough to supply the brain at present. So, the great system throws all this knowledge, theory, and practice, to supply ourselves and move towards equilibrium, or at least keep us in normal balance and that allows us to enjoy a best state of physical, mental, and emotional health and interrelation with the environment.

The great observer and full balance are the task of every day, in a continuous and constant process. If that continuity is lost, it becomes neuronal contraction. Without forgetting that neuronal fuel is the key piece of the super brain's ability in full balance.

Also, if there is no natural or neural fuel, it will end up causing resets. If there is no neural rewiring in a balanced way, the deterioration of the physical, mental, and emotional health of the person is achieved. Therefore, the adjustments that are needed are made when applying the method as neural fuel, since you also access the field of this method that holds all the benefits of applying the formula of the cycle and flow of money, adjusting at the level of neural networks. By giving it that continuity, the results will be shown without generating judgments and expectations.

In the absence of natural and neuronal fuel, diseases tend to appear in the systems in which it is interrelated, in addition therefore it achieves the imbalance of heart-brain-intestines-coccyx. The purpose of this method is that balance is achieved and allows you to have a full life without affecting physical, mental, emotional health and stop creating imbalance in giving, and be a more balanced, gradual, progressive, and continuous process, so staying in balance is living in prosperity.

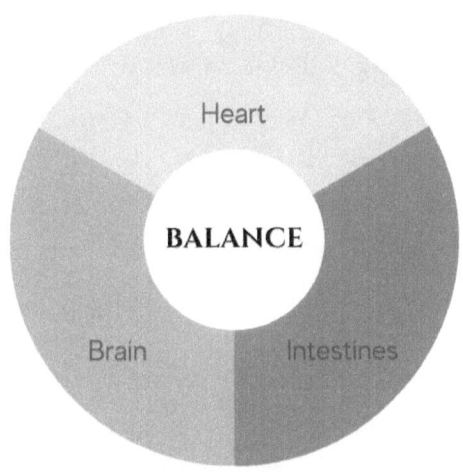

CREATING NEW NEURAL CIRCUITS: GIVE-MONEY-LIGHT

The ability to create new circuits is also called neuroplasticity; To achieve this, the integration of the circuit is carried out: give-money-light.

CREATING NEW NEURAL CIRCUITS

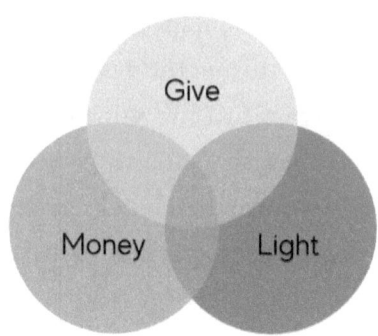

To do this, make the following monthly diagram, where you write in numbers, your income, salaries or fees, expenses or investments, real estate, land, trusts, credits, loans, donations, etc. The column of expenses and investments can be converted into one. Also write down debts, credits, trusts, paid vacations, mortgages, investments, and other expenses.

An expense can be seen as an investment rather than a burden, be it a personal expense or a business expense; the same goes for a debt, which can be interpreted as the amount of light the brain needs to balance the person.

Therefore, to integrate all the above, a sum of income, debts, credits, loans, mortgages, fear, fear systems, belief systems about money, etc. is made. The monthly total of the amount of money in the diagram is the amount of light the brain has needed to stay in balance; this has been the fuel for rewiring the brain and achieving balance with the total amount of giving and this is the network connection.

INCOME AND EXPENSES

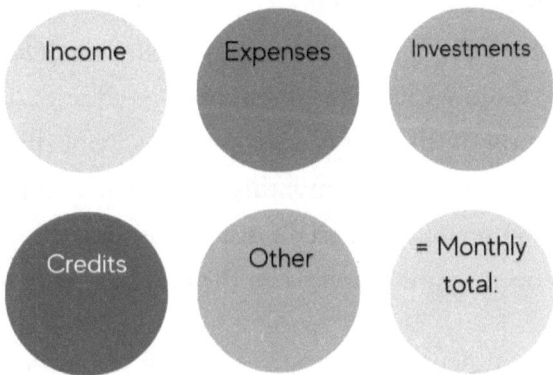

Sometimes there are more credits or loans than income, and that happens because the brain is not supplying itself with natural or neural fuel, uses debt as an amount of light to balance the neuronal potential. So, through this integration (expansion to form the give-money-light circuit in this method), the brain will begin to integrate those credits, debts, and loans, without separation. It is from there that income begins to grow.

With this diagram of income and expenses it is revealed that there is a direct connection with the company or business and with you. Perform every day the exercise of connecting or integrating your company or business; see you from and towards a 5th act or state of harmony, equanimity, great observer as a pillar in your company.

Make this diagram personally, it also applies to companies or businesses. Then, write all this information into a personal timeline, company, or business.

The goal of this diagram is to integrate income and expenses; Connect from the heart with unity without separation. That is, it is to understand the income and expenses without separation in give-money-light. The neuronal expansion integrates the resets that are created within the contraction, in addition to the resets are a function of time, so it is suggested to work this diagram of income and expenditures monthly, since neural adjustments are made to stop seeing debt, credit or loans as something bad, but as what has been required to rewire the brain and stay in balance.

Consequently, neural synchronicity is achieved, which means that there are no longer switched off circuits and they achieve balance in the flow and cycle of money, this translates into fluidity and movement of the neural network system. At the same time, the creation of money in physical representation. From this you will perceive the credit, debts, loans, expenses, investment, mortgage as a loss, but rather, from another point of view and without separation.

As everything is integrated as: debts, credits, or loans, in turn they are transformed, supplied, and disappear, they stop causing the feeling of pain or loss at the time of giving, either to pay or pay them. Expenses will be seen as investments, from profit and joy to you, this fulfills the cycle of giving.

INTEGRATION OF INCOME AND EXPENSES

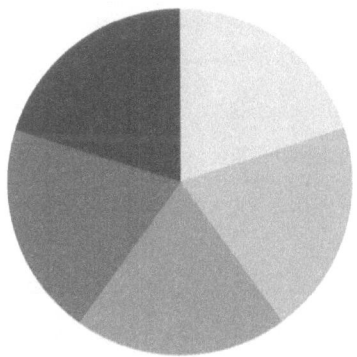

The perspective of what money is integrated; it is no longer seen as a burden. Before this, everything begins to flow from that state of harmony. The brain is rewired to stop seeing spending as something bad and more as an investment; that is when a whole transformation happens in your system. For example, an investment in health is not an expense, it is an investment in well-being and balance.

Our brain will see that nothing is bad, nothing is separate and that everything is an investment in our well-being.

There has to be a transformation from understanding and then that will be transmitted to the environment. When that happens, you start to generate more investment, more income, creating new business opportunities and new networks of friendship, love, effective negotiations and in general, good relationships with the environment.

As a result of the understanding that has been achieved, a state of harmony is generated that will make the system fluence much better with the definition of the quantity or representation of money in all its manifestations. An example could be the companies or businesses that have been born through a credit, mortgage, or loan, and that today have become companies of great international expansion.

All the pieces that have been formed so far integrate this method as fuel, it brings us closer to that balance where it will no longer require credit or debt to supply itself in a natural way, this means that it begins to transform credits, debts, and loans, but not from fear, doubt or from contraction, but from certainty and equanimity. Therefore, the state of the great observer is to live without fear of anything, it is to have everything in a fluid and materialized way.

CHAPTER 5

TIME CYCLES

The origin unites us.

ANA LARA

Time cycles are consciousness, energy, great field, great network system, among others; succession of events, manifestation, seed of life and destiny; it is everything. They have characteristics such as: timelessness, cyclicity, and durability over time.

Time cycles are the creation and union of alternate network systems where you have had life experiences. This refers to uniting all lives in the same line to form time cycles and support balance. It must be considered that the time cycles adjust along the way to travel, the finality is to return to the point of connection (origin) and break.

It is raised in this method, the neural rewiring according to the time cycles, which are part of the money, this means that the resets or neural rewiring are a function of time.

Through the integration of the observer acts and the realities, you can go to the past, present, or future, this means that if you can go, you can observe, anticipate, shorten, lengthen, or extend time, but it has to do with the capabilities of the super brain as a characteristic of achieving the balance of neuronal potential.

Time is in relation to money, sometimes the answers come before the questions, that is, the signs are presented before what happens. For something to happen, some pieces of the puzzle must be moved, that's when the solution is presented.

Time has its characteristic of cyclicity, that is, that some circumstances or situations that have been experienced previously are repeated, anchored, or hosted in the network. Because of this, people in the system report automatically connecting to other networks, either through an event, circumstance, or situation. Therefore, the large field requires neural fuel to balance and stop replicating alternate networks.

Time cycles are closely related to network connection and the brain. The manifestation of these time cycles occurs from 3 times: before, during and after any event or circumstance.

Also, time is closely related to money, since it is about joining all the lines at the same time to form cycles, and this is also the creation of money, creating new neural circuits give-money-light-time.

Learn to navigate (observe) in the time cycles and create new realities, connect with money and love from time cycles. It integrates the definition and understanding of time cycles to create a network connection. The observer, when integrating the 5 realities or 5 acts towards the great observer, can place patterns or keywords in the network system. The above is possible in conjunction with transformative language, use this language mentioned in the previous chapters to manifest and anchor in your corresponding system.

THE GREAT OBSERVER

The large structure of network systems consists of different machines in motion, integrating time cycles. There are many types of machines; As are cells, among them there are machines that take the form of cameras, which take shape in movement, depending on how the eye or observer perceives them, and the neuronal potential in balance. The giving cycle opens the chambers of time cycles in neural network systems.

Reality is already created, it is not thought that creates, and this is because the teleporter (also called a sieve), can recycle and transform all the information in the network, such as thoughts and emotions from the atomic level to molecular. This allowed us to transform everything that was sent to the field of the person and its interrelation with the network or other fields, thoughts, emotions, stimuli, etc. All the above was transformed by the teleporter and connected to the network, this means that everything that reaches this field or network is the contribution of love of people.

The great observer is the multiple possibilities, this proves its existence through the network connection and the observer acts.

Coexisting in other realities is the connection of the past, present, and future; access to the 3 times: before, during and after. This is neural expansion, the totality of all realities happening at the same time.

REALITIES

I am coexisting in other realities; this is the 5th. Act.

ANA LARA

The great observer means multiple realities, so the brain can live one reality in another time, even coexist in other realities. Perceiving alternate realities at the same time, and seen from the great observer, the same event can be replicated and duplicated n times more. Reality is adjustable depending on the environment, such as the space-time set.

The realities are related to the creation of money. Enhancing super brain abilities such as telepathy or teleportation is related to the energy of money, since the latter is related to the cycle of giving birth.

Giving and coexisting in other realities is related to the abilities of the super brain to achieve full balance. Sometimes we condition giving, if this happens, it can fragment or create imbalance in time cycles.

On the other hand, only 3% of the population has access to some type of technology to work and generate the welfare state. 97%

do not know or do not have access to some type of technology. In case studies, it has been seen that only 3% can access some technology to create well-being and of this, only 1.5%, manage to give continuity to support balance, creating the circuit give-money-light and connecting with the state of wholeness in the areas of your life.

In such a way that to achieve the expansion in the transformation of network systems, this is also the integration of realities, it is required that the other 97% can reach the understanding of a new consciousness, live in prosperity and unity; the above is the reason and motive for the existence of this method that aims to integrate neuronal expansion, time cycles, realities to achieve. The balance of the flow and money cycle and this also represent prosperity in all areas of life.

Therefore, although the process of resetting the supercomputer-brain was impossible before, today with the movements of network systems, everything is possible to achieve full balance as human evolution continues.

The existence of other realities is proved through the observer acts and towards the state of the great observer, which also is neuronal expansion, the state of harmony and full balance. It is proposed in this method as seen in the following image: 5 acts, 5 realities; as a new possibility of transformation or new rebirth, given the brain evolution that is happening in an accelerated way day by day.

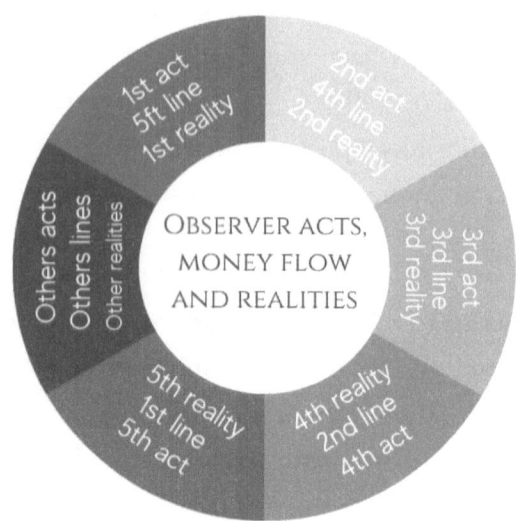

The following audio of the group session is available, accessing the QR:

CHAPTER 6

FORMULA INTEGRATION

This is the formula of the flow and cycle of money that works this method, which aims to work and integrate into your daily life:

Money = Giving (network connection) + neural expansion + time cycles

- Giving: Cycle and principle of giving, known as network connection.
- Neural expansion: Creating the give-money-light circuit.
- Time cycles: Unifies and integrates realities.

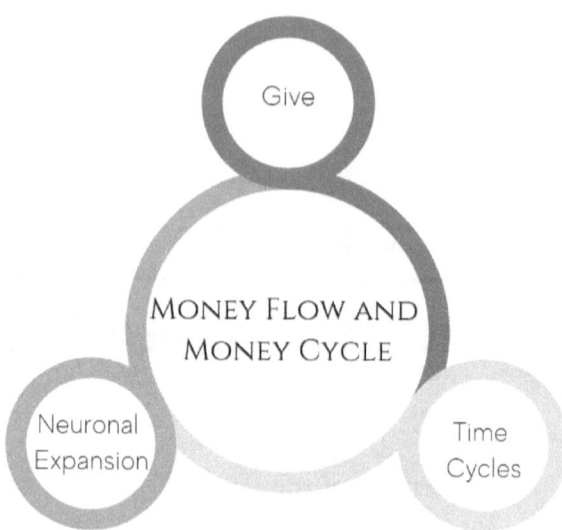

This formula shows that it is synchronized in the field and in the system. Throughout the cycle you must work on the formula for money.

Alternatively, the same field will say that it requires neural fuel, so you can now integrate this method.

Money is light in motion and fluid. Thus, from the great observer, new networks are created where everything is money and light, integrating love and faith. Therefore, when the method is understood, the cycle of giving and living in prosperity is prepared. Materialize the life project, together with the creation of new companies and businesses, because network systems are very abundant.

Answer these questions to continue integrating the formula:

1. Do you know how to integrate the uncertainty of money?
2. Do you measure success by the amount of money?
3. Do you believe that everything is money?
4. If light is money, is money light?
5. Does money push you away or hold you back?
6. Do you believe that money separates?

Continuing with the integration of the theory, non-integrated rewiring can worsen insomnia, neurotransmitter imbalance and lack of oxygen in the blood. So, we must go towards the great networks system to supply the fuel that will make it possible to connect with that transformative language.

Integrating the formula means ceasing to connect with networks of obligation, selfishness, and commitment. In this way, new networks, new potential customers, or loving and abundant people are created; In this way, the system continues its own cycle.

Fueling to achieve full balance is integrated as you advance in the creation and operation of the key, which is the circuit: give-money-light, which is the basis of prosperity.

When events or circumstances are postponed or projects do not occur, an imbalance is created in network systems, because there is no connection or balance for keeping the circuit: give-money-light. When a system of neural networks is fueled, new networks are created where the brain connects, and this refers to being in direct connection with the cycle of giving, which means being in that constant creation of money.

If you work constantly and refuel using this method, you can consolidate your transactions or have effective, successful, and lasting negotiations. The great system shows that the amount of light it supplies is the same amount that is given back.

This is related to multiplication, although giving is not something we expect to multiply, but the system itself multiplies it; with no separation between the creation of money and the representation of the current money we have.

Giving can be described as the whole. So, a practical exercise is to find how we are giving, whether in a relationship, family and/or work. Giving comes from connection with the heart; while giving to the environment is in addition; If the case were to happen where giving goes more towards the environment, an imbalance would be created, and it would be the counterpart.

Observe and ask yourself, have you found and lived in synchronicity with the roles you have had? That is, what situations have you lived in as a couple, business or company that have replicated? The great network system has all the information and when saturated, neuronal contraction is created; This happens when more than two circuits are continuously turned off in the same series or network.

Today entrepreneurs perceive money in the sense of accumulation; what will happen is the fall of the human being, of well-being and of business, because there is no edification in terms of the theory or understanding of the flow and money cycle. That is why you have life experiences, so that it is shown that it is possible to arrive and stay in the state of harmony, to see that the creation of money occurs and manifests itself from the certainty that it is happening.

The cycle of giving could be represented as a sun, which would be the observer. Light can change shape, whether it's bills, houses, food, whatever; this is an abundant river of light is where you can come in and take all that flow of light-money, without stopping it, without accumulating it, because it's a continuous flow. Just take what you need.

You can also supply or give to others who don't have that connection or that ability to go into the river and share that light. We must understand that money is light and that it is something completely different from the concept we have preconceived. The function of neural fuel involves detoxifying and restructuring the entire network system to integrate infinite light.

The great task of the human being is to be able to achieve integration towards unity, couple unit, family unit, organizational unit, business unit, etc. What the great system requires, is that we integrate towards the non-human giving, this is the network connection, from the understanding of neuronal expansion, where the representation of money is not only something physical, for achieve heart-brain-intestines-coccyx coherence. This is the purpose of integrating this method daily, materializing the cycle of giving and sharing in your life plan, together with the creation of new networks, new relationship with the environment, generating abundant, loving, and prosperous clients, which manifests itself in physical, mental, and emotional health and balance.

PROSPERITY

Prosperity is in you and your neurons, as well as in the integration of this method with the formula of the flow and cycle of money. As seen in the following image:

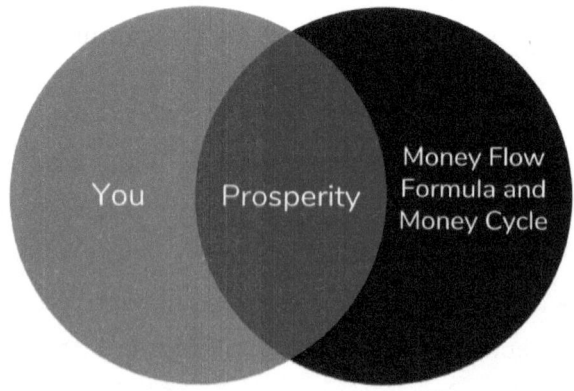

Find the point of balance, transform your brain waves in your day to day through the application of this method as neural fuel: It works as a charger and repairer of your neurons to create new neural circuits give-money-light.

Prosperity is the supply of neural fuel to create the state of harmony and expansion at all levels; It rewires the brain, creates new circuits and neural networks.

Remembering that money is the amount of light and when it reaches its equilibrium, it reaches its maximum potential or neuronal expansion, integrating all realities and time cycles. This is the state of harmony, great observer, or full balance.

The secret is to share and see the world like a great network, everything interconnected with everything without separation. To allow you to live in prosperity, you must think in terms of giving, from networking to the heart vortex. This is the real key.

Listen to the following audio from the group session: prosperity; accessing with the QR:

APPLICATION IN BUSINESS

Believing that only one person can do everything is the separatist vision and ends up falling companies or businesses. Today, it is to generate agreements and contracts as a team. One of the qualities of the super brain in balance is that it can generate networks, groups, or organizations, without fear, without envy, without fear of making mistakes.

A leader in balance knows his work team, their talents, and weaknesses, locates them and potentiates them, giving the role that corresponds to them, observing all the possibilities; He gets going and into action, sees a problem as a possibility, is resilient, and gets ahead with his team. In addition, it has the truly clear ability of the sense of giving and sharing; it creates networks and generates a team of potentialities, generating new systems of business networks.

You can have a business X and become the best seller of X and expand globally.

A leader in imbalance will always need it, it will never be enough; Take remarkably high risks, generate high expectations to generate great results without considering all aspects, events, circumstances, and people.

If you are a natural person and your intention is to do things alone it will not work, since we are in time to create networks, potentialities, or geniuses in balance. Following the theory of the great networks system, if there is no supply of fuel for the creation of networks (equipment), the flow and cycle of money to create the circle: give-money-light ends up falling and this means, the fall of small, medium, and large businesses, corporations, or organizations.

Everything is a network system and has had major influence since the creation of the business from its intention to give, this is the reason things do not happen or end up being chaos. In addition, the fields are not aligned in the intention to give. If there is no equilibrium of neural potential, business tends to disappear or become extinct not because of their products or services but because of their leaders, they do not follow equilibrium or network connection. That is, if in a business, its leaders do not have the corresponding neural fuel, their projects will not be durable over time, they will fall or end up not culminating.

Make and be part of investments with the sense or social purpose of giving and sharing. Allocate your salary or salary to the church, charity, associations, foundations, or create and contribute to an association or foundation; generate network connection. Sometimes you will have situations or circumstances in which the ultimate is to be the great observer, to stop seeing guilt, frustration, selfishness or to feel some feeling opposed to love when it is the main teaching.

That your life project is give-money-light-share, that your social purpose is giving and sharing. Associations and foundations contribute to societies. This is to repair the neural network system and create the circuit: give-money-light. What separates us is egoism, which is also a state of human consciousness.

The end of gambling can occur if they are not aligned with the intention of giving, because the algorithm has another purpose of giving and sharing. Everything that accumulates to receive more, today is uncertain, since they have the purpose of accumulating and by entering those accumulation systems in some way it relates to the lower levels of neuronal contraction.

The result of exposure to neuronal contraction are low frequencies such as judgments and expectations that deplete the neural network system and the immune system.

The process of confusion, doubt, and uncertainty results in hooking the field and this is the previous process of equilibrium. If money fulfills its function of giving and sharing, light is accessed. Active and passive, everything is light without separation. In your business and investments train your work team, partners, shareholders, to achieve the super brain capacity, harmonious state, equanimous; that your purpose is to give and share as a team, to achieve balance, equilibrium, and prosperity.

Currently, a new stage of expansion is proposed, where the system provides this theory to understand how they work and create new neural circuits. The answer comes at the time it is needed, the key is to keep us in balance, having the fuel to supply and thus make repairs to the corresponding neural network systems to create the circuit: give-money-light. That is where integration happens.

Today, staying in balance is possible under the understanding and continuous integration of this method as a fuel supplier for repairs to the deterioration of the neural network system. The key is to stay in balance to be able to connect and achieve continuity.

Money is in all systems and is part of the whole, but in theory, money is not only the mind, it is what we know as physical or circulating. It is common to believe that to accumulate more money you have to accumulate more light, but it is a mistake since light cannot be accumulated, since it expands, flows and is continuous.

You are the field; the system and you are the whole party. If you cannot sustain or keep the amount of light-money in your business, circumstance, event, or situation in balance to connect with other fields and systems, things, projects, or businesses will not happen. The answer to achieve this is to keep the balance of neuronal potential, this is to connect with all fields and systems that have a frequency which are abundant from neuronal expansion.

The key is the heart-brain-intestines-tailbone balance to connect with the abundant business fields to achieve effective and lasting negotiations over time. It is unimaginable that the human brain can access events, circumstances, interrelated people in other systems, networks, organizations, institutions. The great challenge of the human being is to stay in balance to achieve the cycle of giving.

Nowadays, some businesses want to open, since people do not have a foundation built on money and that makes a big difference.

There are basic characteristics that people can present in this case: addiction, excessive confusion, doubt, uncertainty, fear, fear, trauma, among others. Family businesses are the ones that present the most conflicts, because the roles are not well defined, in addition money can have a meaning or relationship with any family member from the ancestral system or lineage.

Understanding how money works is the main basis so that it can be achieved to materialize 100% and that these negotiations, work projects or relationships with the environment, are lasting over time and with the environment. The impact of money as a core part of our lives is then seen.

In the genetic code, there are belief systems about money; examples such as: money separates, money is not equal to all, everything is money, among others. Therefore, this method was born. Balance is a constant, continuous, and progressive process, in such a way that you achieve a connection with money-give-light and neural networks, which will allow the flow and cycle of money.

Neural resets, on the other hand, are losses, deaths, illnesses, and another changes, any near-death experience, among others. Money exists to be an instrument and achieves that full balance.

A foundation or association works differently in country X than in country Y. It is non-profit but requires the money to launch its projects and programs, the money is the vehicle to realize the social goals of the foundation or association.

Giving and receiving can be non-linear, this means that, if you are giving your way back, receiving can come from various sources; this is one of the benefits of network connection.

Achieve balance, even if you do not realize that you are in that direct connection and you are taking your entire work team or your whole family to that state of harmony or equanimity towards the great observer. That is why there are movements, changes, transformation; all in compensation for giving what is being executed.

This implies questioning how you can save without generating judgments and expectations, and that does not diminish your network system either. Investments have been frowned upon, but investment is given and generated. When you integrate all this, the brain enters an expansive process that is known as neuronal expansion and with that you will notice that you stop being afraid of what lives, what money is. Really think about enjoying living, start seeing everything as a business and as a possibility. Talking about business is also talking about giving and sharing.

If seen expansively, businesses and networks are generated where the process of giving is in continuous flux. It is perceived that the amount of light is entering, the amount of money and new businesses are being generated that supply employment to other families; that is precisely the process of giving. Generate investments that in turn create new networks, there is giving, through the creation of new companies, businesses, investment projects, organizations, foundations, etc. It must be understood that money must be in motion and not remain stagnant or accumulated, because that breaks the cycle, as already mentioned before.

The way to generate new networks is to have a business plan to give and share. Having an investment is supplying because there is the process of giving, in salaries, wages, investment advantages, among others; that continues to be expansive until creating network connection under a scheme of giving that is equal amount of light to amount of money. Generate a company where there is a constant flow of money: inputs and outputs; It is also the fuel to give and share.

In the absence of natural fuel, the priority is to have the neural fuel to create the network connection. What breaks the cycle of giving is the duty to be, to have to be commitment, sacrifice, and obligation.

Then, from the moment those red spots begin to appear, various systems such as the immune system begin to be depleted. So, the way to have that balance is to understand how human giving and non-human giving work.

Money has the function of giving. Now, giving that is not human can be seen as network connection, which will be built based on human giving and all-natural fuel, as well as neural fuel (this method) to get there. Therefore, a rewiring of the network system is proposed, so that it can understand that movement of human giving to non-human giving, which is the creation of light, money, network connection, brain-heart-intestines-tailbone balance.

Therefore, adjustments are made from the stage of the anteroom, even before reading this book, during and after reading it. The path is like network connection, non-human giving. It's like climbing a step through the human daft and in the process the other stairs. The result manifests itself in a full understanding, but this time, in a conscious way.

Expectations break the cycles of giving. Understand that giving is also receiving. As in family businesses where there are conflicts and, in the relationship, the roles are not well defined, as this method applicable to businesses is worked, fuel will be supplied and make role adjustments integrated, congruent with the balance of give-money-light and network connection.

The same system will adjust so that these roles can be integrated into businesses, and relationships. So, the only way to achieve balance as a couple is in the integration or understanding of what it is to give and share well-defined and integrated roles.

When you do not have well-defined roles, things do not happen, whether with people or business, because the roles are not well defined and integrated. There is a relationship between switched off circuits, the flow of money and non-integrated roles. Therefore, if we work with this method, it is more likely that our businesses will be abundant, durable, and enduring over time.

On the other hand, when an expectation is generated, it can cut off the fluidity that the neural network system has in connection with our brain. This could be interpreted as a computer where, over time, it presents a slowness of the system because the brain has no fuel to function. As this flow is encouraged, it has consequences and effects on the central nervous system, and on the neural networks system, where there is a direct connection with the businesses.

Therefore, people must integrate, understand, and connect directly with the fields of these companies and thriving businesses. If the person does not work, his own balance, you will not be able to access or connect easily with these fields. Therefore, the person must stock up on fuel to support their full balance: heart-brain-intestines-coccyx.

All fields are very abundant, as well as all areas and businesses. We have worked on annual projections of businesses, where people visualize or project well below what these fields reveal of these same businesses, since they are prosperous and expansive in their entirety.

Staying in balance means light, money, but it is not properly giving money, but it is non-human giving turned into human giving. It is to generate that state of harmony in human giving. Before receiving it is giving and creating, connecting with that space or that state of harmony or joy that creates the process of giving, which is worked day by day, giving and sharing.

To be precise, giving will be the first step to move the machinery along with this method as neural fuel, which will make us move to the curve of non-human giving. Money is going to manifest itself in a relationship of equilibrium and the representation of what we know today as money.

Money is created in network systems, for that reason it will never lack anyone, because it is working in the give-light cycle.

With this understanding, money is created in these systems, to achieve materialization in network connection in a constant, lasting, and continuous way in relations with the environment and businesses. The human being must be open to continue advancing and evolving day by day because living without generating the state of prosperity will cause burdens in the system, create more resistance, more systems crossing (neuronal traffic).

The secret to a full life is to achieve balance in giving, which is the creation of the circuit: give-money-light, prosperity, physical, mental, emotional health, and business. Make and be part of investments, creating new businesses with the sense and social purpose of giving and sharing.

CONCLUSION

Neuron is the creation or flow of life, the intention of the formula of the cycle and flow of money is the creation of life, it is the creation of new neurons that promote balance and balance. The neuron has to do with the levels or degrees of the neural network system and this with money.

Our task and great mission are that our acts manage to create and generate light, this is the creation of the circuit: to give-money-light and achieve the harmonious, coherent, and equitable state. Love is money, money is love, love is giving, giving is money, money is light, light is love. The fields are abundant, what is needed is that the person connects with the coherent state, state of harmony and balance.

The principle of giving is money, money is the principle of giving. Money is light, it is unlimited and inexhaustible as the inexhaustible source of light. If money is giving and light, forever is, already is, has been and will be. Money has been conceived separately from the process of giving when it is reciprocity, that is, money is an integrating process of consciousness, money is the deep ability of giving.

Commitment, obligation, and duty break the cycle of giving, the state of equilibrium is the relationship of money and neural networks. If less money is perceived, it is because a new cycle, renaissance or creation of new circuits in network systems is coming, this is the time to that comes the neural fuel into action.

Gambling will fall because it does not have the characteristics of the integration of the formula of the flow and cycle of money and in relation to the times cycles such as durability since its creation.

Not having the neural fuel can deplete the neural network system. There is a relationship between fueling and the flow of money. The disease is equal to the lack of neuronal fuel.

Various factors create and generate neuronal contraction, this occurs through the creation of fear, fear, extreme confusion, and doubt, can reduce physical, mental, emotional, energetic, spiritual health, etc., to prevent the network connection from being achieved and develop all the abilities of every human being to have a full life, this is the perfect and harmonious balance.

Money can be created on network connection, and this is the new way to create light. Less light, less circulation, flow of life, less money, less oxygen in network connection.

MONEY NEURONS

Money is not possession or wealth, it is not material things, but neural potential. The network connection increases or decreases along with the neural potential. Money is proportional to the light that is integrated into daily life.

To repair the degrees of distortions or alterations, bioshock or short circuits it is possible that they are repaired through the supply of neuronal fuel. You become the observer practitioner in the field and allow the movement and adjustment of networks, which is to go from contraction to expansion.

The 5th act is a new frequency or new state of consciousness, as we advance neuronally if the neuronal fuel is not supplied, the resets or rewiring increase. The lowest levels, or the first acts and the relationship with the greater number of resets or rewiring neuronal deteriorates towards the disease. That is, the greater number of bioshock or short circuits is related to addictions, diseases, and major and frequent neuronal rewiring.

Contraction is the disease, it is separation, it is neuronal contraction, it is where other networks are found: sexual, drugs, addictions.

The contraction can generate neurodegenerative and cardiovascular diseases, for women cervical cancer and for men erectile dysfunction. Alteration in the thyroid glands, parathyroid and thymus. Sleep disturbance, brain-heart disconnection, postpartum depression, trauma, panic attacks, myocardial infarction or cardiac arrest, cerebral infarctions.

The great observer is the expanded part of the observer; Reality is already created; it is not your thought that creates. The great observer is the multiple possibilities, the multiple dimensions, this is verified with the existence of the great observer through the network connection and the same acts. Let your neural fuel be every day, integrating the formula of the cycle and flow of money.

The connectivity model of neural network systems is proposed, that is, the application of fuel in a massive way to integrate the formula of the cycle and flow of money, in the project of "The Crystal City" and this can be measured by the Neuroakashic® crystals technology system applied to the crystal cities, the new humanity. You want to know more about this, access with this QR code:

The Crystal City

RECOMMENDED READING

Lara, Ana Silvia; Neuroakashic® the great observer, a neuroscience progress; Balboa Press; 2020, USA.

Lara, Ana Silvia et al; Emotional health, anxiety, depression and stress, vol. #5; Summarium, collective construction of knowledge, 2022, USA

GLOSSARY

DNA: Deoxyribonucleic acid (DNA) is the molecule that carries genetic information, like a supercomputer.

Bioshock: Process of non-assimilation of events, circumstances or situations creating an alteration in the neural network system.

Bilocation: Term used to describe a paranormal, supernatural, or divine phenomenon. According to which an object or person would be in two unusual places at the same time.

Field n+1: The sum of groupings of neurons.

Neural fuel: Works as a charger or gasoline to repair circuits, bioshocks, short circuits or deterioration in network systems.

Consciousness: Level, state, or degree that certain characteristics are attributed to each other.

Networking: A way of calling the ability to give, in connection with the brain and heart.

Distortion: Characteristic of alteration in the neural network system.

Equanimous: Characteristic of being in a state without judgment or expectation, being without any physical, mental, or emotional alteration.

Fibonacci: Code formed by a series of numbers represented as an image that reveals a movement or adjustment; It is seen as a quantum spiral found throughout nature.

Photonics: They are the particles formed of light.

Great system: It is the sum of all systems, also called large field, great observer, among others.

Neuron: Cell of the nervous system; it is the basis and creation of life.

Neurotransmitters: They function as mediators to send information from one neuron to another.

Neuronal potential: Also called action potential, those waves of electrical discharges that travel from the nucleus of the cell membrane.

Reset: Return to its original state.

Teleporter: Also called sieve; can recycle and transform all information that exist in the system of networks, such as thoughts and emotions from atomic to molecular level.

Vortex: Energy center or energy space.

ABOUT THE AUTHOR

ANA SILVIA LARA

Ana Silvia Lara is an author, lecturer and international instructor, certified consultant in business and human rights. She has other studies in neuroscience, molecular biology, genetics, stress management and trauma.

She has leadership, creativity, and negotiation skills. She was born in the city of Comitán de Domínguez, Chiapas, Mexico, currently lives with her family in California. She has a degree in Economics from the Popular Autonomous University of Puebla (UPAEP) Mexico.

She wrote the book "*Neuroakashic®* the *great observer, an advance in neurosciences*", Spanish and English version and co-author of *the* best seller *"Anxiety, stress and depression, summarium vol. 5"*, author of the best-seller book in Spanish of *"Money neurons, practical method to live in prosperity"*. She has taken part in various interviews and conferences internationally on radio, TV, and online programs.

It has managed to impact for more than 14 years, in thousands of people, training practitioners and facilitators, sharing sessions, classes and individual, groups and businesses certifications.

Currently as director and co-founder of The Crystal City non-profit organization in California, she teaches online modality and travels to other countries to transmit, expand and create with the Neuroakashic® crystals technology system certification applied to the construction of the new crystal cities to maintain the state of full balance, cerebral and cardiac coherence, harmony, well-being, balance and unite families in the new crystal cities, the new humanity.

Contact us:

Web: www.anasilvialara.com

Email: info@anasilvialara.com

Mobile: +1 786 281 04 65

Country: United States

facebook.com/ anasilvialaraa instagram.com/anasilvialara

linkedin.com/in/ana-silvia-lara

youtube.com/@AnaSilviaLara

www.ingramcontent.com/pod-product-compliance
Lightning Source LLC
Chambersburg PA
CBHW020444220526
45464CB00002B/848